Kids First Publishing, LLC
www.jeff-gray-books.com

Thanks to the secondary students and staff at Lighthouse Primary and Secondary School in the Republic of Mauritius. The situations in this book are unrelated to the staff and students in the illustrations. The students and staff depicted are friends that agreed to help me with this project. A special thanks to Adam Amberg for organizing the photos and to Rahul Subrun for taking amazing photos. Thanks Susanna Dalais for being an Eats, Shoots & Leaves expert. Thank you Elize Koekemoer for your diligence in creating the book design. Thanks to my three daughters, Amanda, Haley and Vivian for the privilege of being your dad. Finally, a special thanks to my wife, Denise, for loving me enough to stick with me through thick and thin. I am a blessed man.

If He Only Knew Me...

If he only knew that I'm living in a car around the corner from the school and that's why I keep falling asleep in class. I'm not the cleanest kid in class but I do the best I can.

If He Only Knew Me...

If he only knew that humiliating us doesn't make us stronger. It makes us bitter.

If He Only Knew Me...

If he only knew that my uncle hurts me when my parents aren't home, he would stop putting his hands on me.

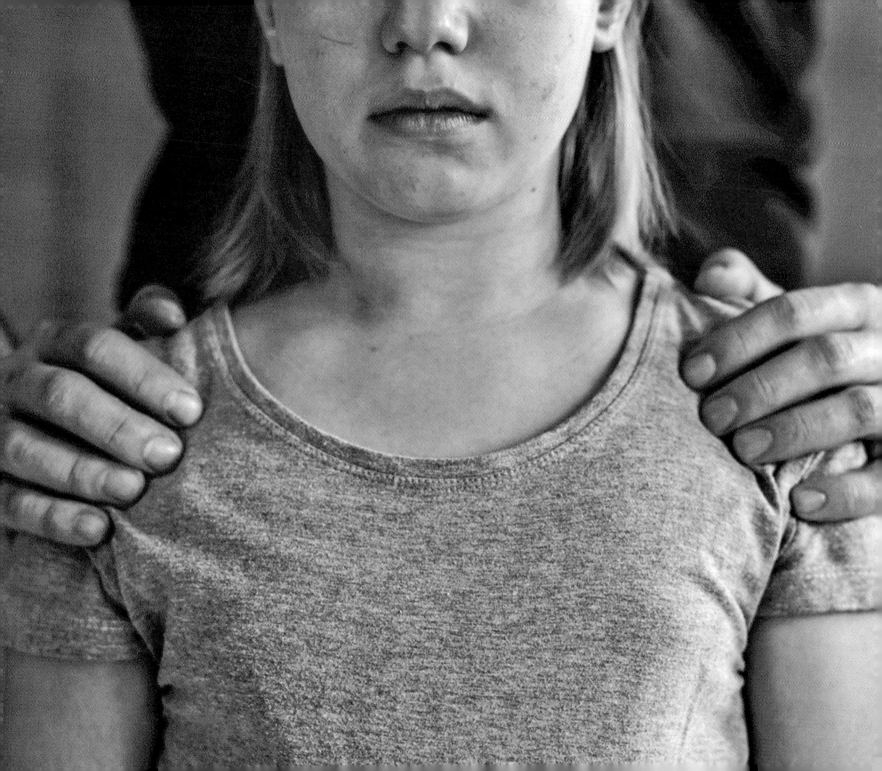

If He Only Knew Me...

If he only knew that the girls bully in a different way than the boys, he would break up the small groups of whisperers in our class.

If He Only Knew Me...

If he only knew that I've been cutting myself to cope with the pain that I feel, he'd stop making jokes about my sweatshirt in the heat of August.

If He Only Knew Me...

If he only knew that my house is being condemned by the city, he'd stop talking about his four-bedroom house and hot tub during class.

If He Only Knew Me...

If he only knew that we don't want to hear about the X's and O's of Friday night's football game. X's and O's don't matter on the ACT. Teach me X and Y- I'm waiting.

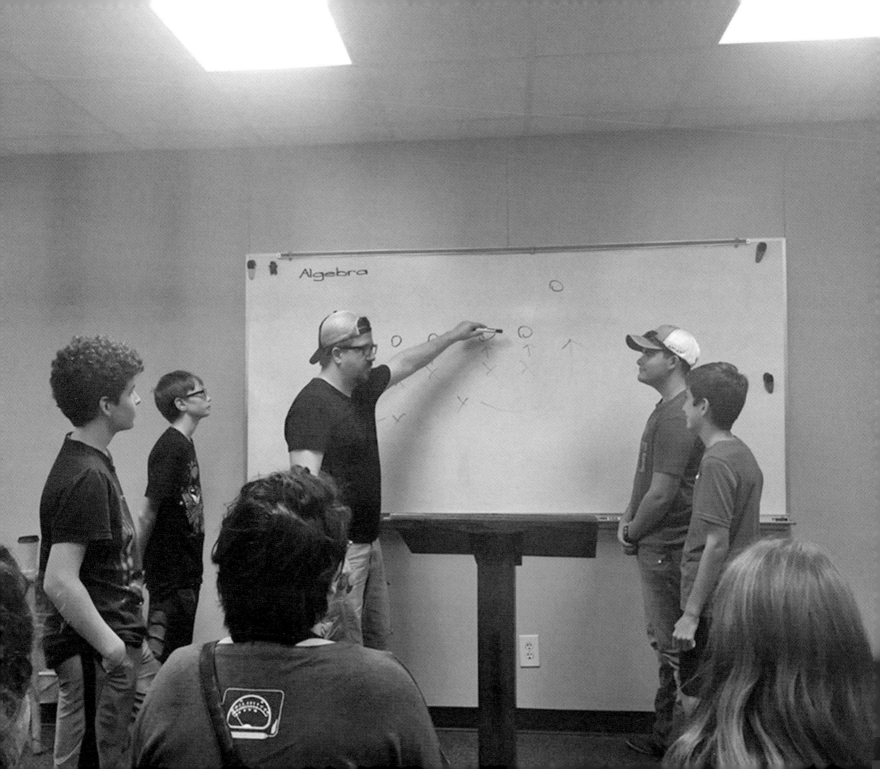

If He Only Knew Me...

If he only knew that all the kids notice the way he stares at the pretty girls he'd stop doing that. It's nasty. He could be her grand-daddy!

Personal Experience: My daughter attended a boarding school in Kenya while we lived abroad. We returned to the USA and enrolled her in the local high school. At the end of one of her English classes, she approached the teacher to ask, "How long should my essay be for this assignment." The teacher's response: "Your essay should be like a skirt: long enough to cover all the important parts but short enough to keep me interested." As you can imagine, the school received a visit from me that afternoon.

If He Only Knew Me...

If he only knew that political views are personal and if he wants to teach the class regarding his views, he needs a different classroom...this is the AP Biology.

If He Only Knew Me...

If he only knew that his jokes about immigrants aren't funny to me. My family came to America out of civil war. We almost died.

If He Only Knew Me...

If he only knew that I had two little sisters and one little brother, and my mom works two jobs. She's never home. I take care of everything at home. I'm tired. I wish he'd stop telling me to be responsible. Right now, I don't need a lecture, I need help.

If He Only Knew Me...

If he only knew that I've considered ending my life multiple times this year, he would ask if I'm OK. My grades have dropped from A's to D's, I've missed school five times in three weeks, I haven't combed my hair in a month. I just don't know how to ask for help.
Does anyone care?

If He Only Knew Me...

If he only knew that I don't come to school events at night because in my neighborhood that's when people get shot. Police won't even come to our neighborhood at night.

He shouldn't offer bonus points for those that attend because ten points on my next test aren't worth a bullet to the head!

If He Only Knew Me...

If he only knew that I'd rather get a root canal than sit through his class. I think he hates teaching as much as we hate being in his class.
At least the dentist seems like he cares.

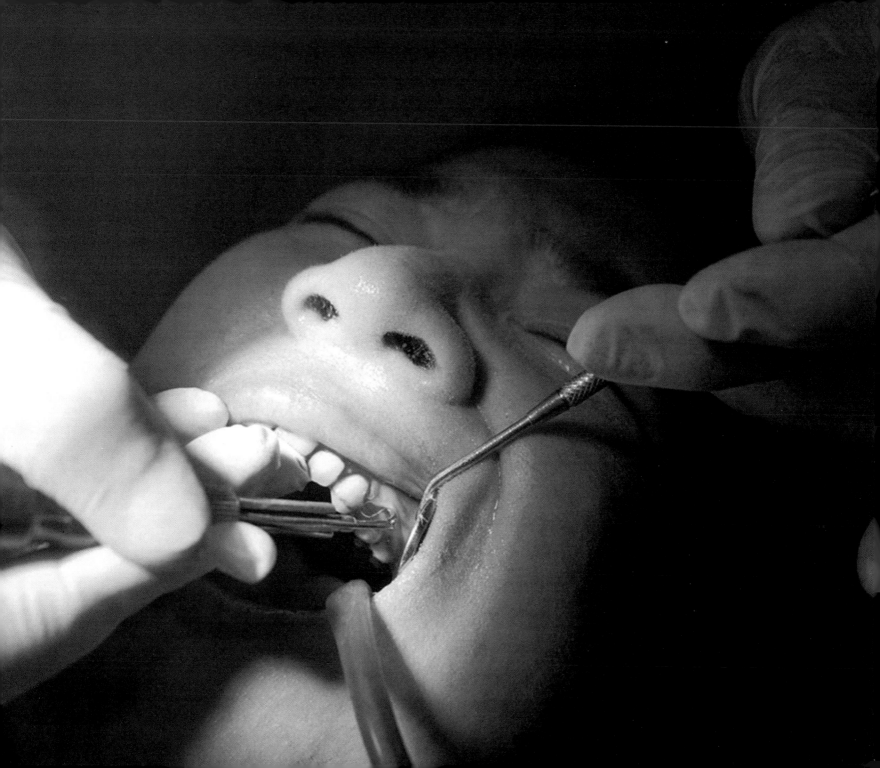

If He Only Knew Me...

If he only knew that my boyfriend seems really nice, but he hits me when he's angry. I'm afraid of him and I don't know what to do.

If He Only Knew Me...

If he only knew that I purge every day after lunch because I hate myself, he would try to help me. It seems like everyone knows but my teachers.

If He Only Knew Me...

He would help me.

You are important and you matter.

Your feelings matter.

Your voice matters.

Your story matters.

Your life matters.

Always and forever...

This is the message that girls should receive from us. Not only in our words but in our actions.